THE TURNING POINT

LEADER GUIDE

Eight Encounters with Jesus That Will Change Your Life

DR. ALLEN HUNT

Dynamic Catholic

Published by Beacon Publishing

Study Guide ISBN: 978-1-929266-62-3
Leader Guide ISBN: 978-1-929266-92-0
DVD ISBN: 978-1-929266-97-5

Design by Jessica Amsberry

Library of Congress Cataloging-in-Publication Data
Names: Hunt, Allen Rhea, 1964- author.
Title: The Turning Point : Eight Encounters with Jesus That Will Change Your Life / Dr. Allen R. Hunt.
Description: North Palm Beach : Beacon Publishing, 2017.
Identifiers: LCCN 2017016400 | ISBN 9781929266623 (softcover)
Subjects: LCSH: Bible. John--Textbooks. | Jesus Christ--Friends and associates--Textbooks.
Classification: LCC BS2616 .H77 2017 | DDC 226.5/092--dc23
LC record available at https://lccn.loc.gov/2017016400

For more information on this title or other books and CDs available through the Dynamic Catholic Book Program, please visit www.DynamicCatholic.com.

The Dynamic Catholic Institute
5081 Olympic Blvd • Erlanger • Kentucky • 41018
Phone: 1-859-980-7900
Email: info@DynamicCatholic.com

FIRST EDITION
First printing, January 2018

Printed in the United States of America

Table of Contents

OUR GOAL:
A PERSONAL RELATIONSHIP WITH JESUS CHRIST

Man, himself created in the "image of God" [is] called to a personal relationship with God.

Catechism of the Catholic Church, 299

Leader's Task

The leader of the group should:

1. Prepare ahead of time how you plan to handle each session. It may not be possible each week to discuss everything in full detail. Feel free to select the areas and questions you think will be most meaningful and those for which you have sufficient time.

2. With that in mind, one excellent way to open the group discussion each session might be asking one of the following two open-ended questions:

    a. How did God speak to you personally through the homework and preparation time this week?
    b. How did Allen's talk on the DVD speak to you personally today?

3. Create a setting of openness, honesty, and warmth. We are in this together. We are all on the same team. God has made us for each other, to encourage and strengthen one another in our time together.

    - When it comes to sharing personal experiences, the leader will often be the first person to share in order to set the tone for a safe environment.

    - Invite the group to make a covenant that all discussions will remain private and not be shared outside the group. This will encourage people to be honest and real in their comments rather than feeling the need to be guarded.

4. Facilitate the discussion. Work to ensure that each member who desires to share has the opportunity to do so, and also that no single member dominates all the talking.

5. If you are leading a group of more than ten people, it will be helpful to break the group into smaller subsets of five or six for the discussion time. This will create smaller, more intimate settings where people feel more comfortable being open and sharing their insights. It is also recommended that you place men and women in separate groups when possible. This tends to increase participation and maintain healthy boundaries.

6. Keep the focus of the group. Prevent conversation from wandering into areas of academic debate, personal disputes, or unrelated subjects. Also, be comfortable with not being able to answer every question.

7. Keep the group to the maximum seventy-five-minute time commitment. This is very important. Manage the time allotted to achieve the greatest conversation and learning setting possible.

8. Arrive early to each session. Ensure that the meeting space is ready when members arrive and that any materials are already prepared (e.g., the computer, projector, and projector screen). Be sure the lights are on, the chairs are arranged, and any coffee or water bottles are set out and available.

The Group Session (Maximum Seventy-Five Minutes)

You will guide the group each week using the following format:

1. **Welcome and Announcements (five minutes)**
   Keep these brief. Emphasize why we are gathering: to encourage one another as we seek an encounter with Jesus Christ.

2. **Opening Prayer (five minutes)**
   Lead the group in praying aloud the opening prayer from Thomas Merton (found in the inside front cover of the Study Guide).

3. **Watch DVD and Complete DVD Response Sheet (twenty to thirty minutes)**
   - Read aloud the Scripture passage for "This Week's Encounter" to set the stage for the DVD and discussion to follow. Then begin playing the DVD talk.
   - Instruct the participants to complete their own DVD Response Sheets and take notes during Allen's video talk about the Gospel of John.

4. **Small Group Discussion (thirty minutes)**
   Study Guide and Readings
   - Feel free to focus on the questions you think will make for the most helpful session.
   - Consider beginning with the open-ended question suggested in number three on the previous page.
   - Included in this Leader Guide are some observations and suggestions for leading the discussion around the study questions. These suggestions are highlighted in script font so that you can easily identify them in this Guide.

- Facilitate the conversation as you lead the group through the discussion questions they will have completed before arriving. It is important to emphasize to the participants each week the need to prepare ahead of time so that the group can benefit the most from its time together.
- Each week's questions are based on the readings from John's Gospel and will also incorporate personal reflection. Discussion will center on the "This Week's Encounter" passage and related study questions from John.
- You do not need to lead a conversation around the "Go Deeper" or "Just for You" sections. Participants will do those reflections on their own as they prepare each week.
- Feel free also to incorporate prayer and encouragement in the group as much as you are comfortable.

5. **Closing Prayer (five minutes)**
   End the session by leading the group in praying aloud the Prayer of a Dynamic Catholic (found in the inside back cover of the Study Guide).

First Meeting—Suggestions for Getting Acquainted

When the group gathers for the first time, remind them that we are here to encourage one another to learn and to grow. God made us to be together as a community to bear one another's burdens and to support one another in becoming the-best-versions-of-ourselves. Our goal is to pray and to stimulate each other to excellence as we seek an encounter with Jesus Christ.

At the first meeting, please do the following:

1. Have each person introduce himself or herself with a full name and the name by which he or she likes to be called. Name tags are very important for the first meeting as well as the three meetings thereafter. Encourage each person to make a list of names in his or her Study Guide. This will be a helpful way to remember one another.

2. Review the materials and give a brief overview of the process:
   - We'll spend nine weeks together, including this first session.
   - We'll spend a maximum of seventy-five minutes together each time.
   - We will start and end on time.
   - Daily preparation is essential. Each participant will get the most from this study by coming to the group session fully prepared and ready.
   - Ask if there are questions about the study or the directions.
   - Be sure the reading assignment is clear for the next lesson.

3. Prayer will be the central ingredient of this group's life together. Invite members to begin praying for the other people in the group since they have already written their names in the Study Guide.

SESSION ONE:

STUDY OVERVIEW

KEY VERSE:

But these are written that you may believe that Jesus is the Christ, the Son of God, and that believing you may have life in His name. (John 20:31)

Gospel of John: Our Process

Over these nine weeks, we will study and discuss eight personal encounters with Jesus in John's Gospel. Here is how we will prepare for each week:

I. Preparation for the Group Session

Each week, you will have **two** reading assignments from the Gospel of John.

First, you will read and study in detail one passage that shares an encounter with Jesus. Your weekly preparation for the group gathering (Sections I, II, and III) will guide you to reflect on this single passage.

Each group session will then focus on that one passage from John's Gospel to help you dive deeper into a personal encounter with Jesus. Our goal will be to study one person's experience with Jesus in order to enrich our own relationship with Him. In preparation for the weekly group sessions, please complete the appropriate section of the Study Guide on your own.

In order to get the most out of your weekly preparation, you will find it helpful to set aside about fifteen minutes each day to work on the Study Guide. Completion of each week's full section of the Study Guide will take about ninety minutes. You will quickly discover that the more intentionally and thoroughly you prepare, the more rewarding your experience will be. God will honor your diligence and work and reveal Himself to you in new ways.

We recommend that you begin your preparation and reading time each day with prayer. Ask God to open your eyes, ears, and heart to His voice in Sacred Scripture as you read. We suggest using the Dynamic Catholic Prayer Process, which is provided for you on page 62.

Second, you are also encouraged to read three full chapters of the Gospel of John each week in order to read through the entire Gospel (there are twenty-one chapters in total). This "Go Deeper" portion of the study (Section IV) will give you the fullest experience possible. By reading the entire Gospel, you will get a sense of the whole picture that John is painting. Taking the time to read the entire Gospel will supplement the regular weekly preparation and group discussion times. This additional reading will be for your own personal journey and will not be discussed directly in the group session.

To guide you, in the workbook, each week's "Go Deeper" section will provide the three chapters to read and the simple journal question for you to reflect on: "What one thing did God say to you in this chapter?" By the end of the study, you will have gathered twenty-one touchstone reflections to refer back to from your own journey through each chapter of John's Gospel.

II. Group Session (approximately seventy-five minutes)

You will need your Study Guide and Bible for each group session.

1. **Announcements** (five minutes)

2. **Opening Prayer** (five minutes)
   Prayer by Thomas Merton (found on the inside front cover)

3. **Watch the DVD and use the DVD Response Sheet for notes** (twenty minutes).

4. **Small group discussion** (twenty to thirty minutes)
   Study Guide and Readings
   Prayer and Encouragement

5. **Closing Prayer** (five minutes)
   Prayer of a Dynamic Catholic (found on the inside back cover)

III. Resources

- *The Turning Point: Eight Encounters with Jesus That Will Change Your Life*
- Bible. You can purchase The New Testament (Revised Standard Version—Catholic Edition) from DynamicCatholic.com.

NOTE: All Scripture references in *The Turning Point* are from the Revised Standard Version, Catholic Edition (RSV-CE), unless otherwise noted. The study's author has chosen to capitalize references to the name of God in the translation printed in the study guide.

SESSION ONE: INTRODUCTORY GROUP SESSION

Beginning the Journey Together

GROUP SHARING

This first session is designed to help build a sense of trust and community in the participants. Please spend the first twenty minutes or so on these group sharing questions. In the future lessons, the group discussion time will focus on the readings from the Gospel of John.

Since many groups will not receive the Study Guide until the first gathering, there is no assigned reading for this first session. As the Group Leader, you will lay the foundation for the study and then lead the group in the discussion questions and DVD viewing included at the end of this overview.

1. **Who are you?** Share your name and one thing about yourself no one else in the room knows.

2. **Why are you here?** What are your hopes for this study and the group sessions?

3. **What one area of your life do you hope is most impacted by studying the Gospel of John?**

JOURNAL

How is life? Reflect on what's working and what's not working in your life.

Encourage the participants to use the remaining ten minutes to journal. Remind them that they will not need to share these answers aloud and that they may continue journaling when they get home. The journal time is designed to foster the encounter with Christ.

You will also want to encourage them to return to this lesson and read the Introduction, Setting and Style section, and Layout section, so that they have a fuller picture of the Gospel of John as the study begins.

Jesus has answers to your questions, and He offers you the best way to live. Together we will seek Him in our preparation and in these sessions. We will pray for one another and encourage each other forward. May our journeys be filled with Jesus' grace.

SESSION TWO:

THE WORLD ENCOUNTERS JESUS

KEY VERSE:

And the Word became flesh and dwelt among us, full of grace and truth; we have beheld His glory, glory as of the only Son from the Father. (John 1:14)

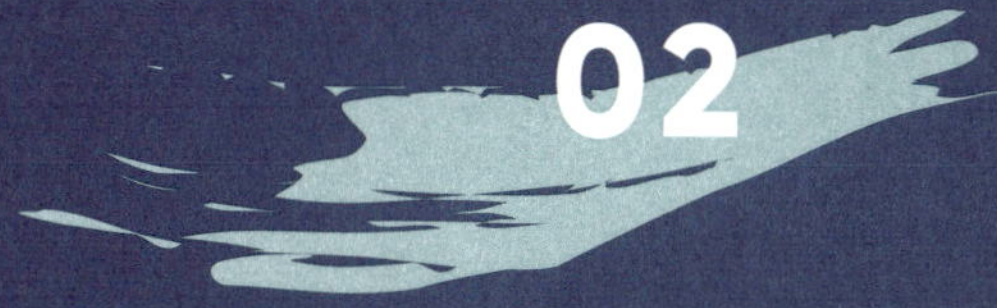

II. This Week's Encounter—John 1:1–18

These verses form the Prologue to the Gospel of John.

Answer the following questions to help you reflect on what you read in John 1:1–18 of the Fourth Gospel. **TIP: Circle the questions you find the most interesting or difficult and discuss them with your group at the next session.**

1. The Gospel of John starts with "In the beginning . . ." Compare that to Genesis 1:1. Why do you think John chose to use that phrase?

Notice how Genesis starts in the beginning as God prepares to create. Notice how John takes us all the way back to that beginning since verses two and three of John chapter one indicate that Jesus, The Word, was with God in the beginning and that all things were made through Him. John is taking us back to the beginning and showing how Jesus is God and has always been.

This session will feel a bit different from the others in this study. These first verses in the Gospel of John do not describe one encounter with Jesus so much as they set the stage for all the encounters to come. John himself has had a deeply personal experience with Christ, but he believes it is important to start with the biggest question of all: Who is Jesus?

2. In verses one and fourteen, John describes Jesus as the "Word." The Greek word for that is *Logos*. Here it means "God's speech," or God revealing Himself to the world in Jesus. To Greeks, *Logos* was more than just a spoken word—it was the divine reason that holds the entire universe together, giving all creation order and structure. Greeks also used this term to describe the link between our human minds and the mind of God.

   What are some reasons you think John started with this "Word of God" concept rather than with the stories of the Annunciation to Mary or the birth of Jesus in Bethlehem?

   The Gospel of John is much more philosophical in nature than the other Gospels. John is painting the really big picture for us, giving us a cosmic perspective of Jesus.

3. This is our key verse for the session:

   And the Word became flesh and dwelt among us,
   full of grace and truth; we have beheld His glory,
   glory as of the only Son from the Father.
   (John 1:14)

   Have you heard this verse before?

   This is Allen's favorite verse in the entire Bible. Why do you think he likes it so much?

   For me, this verse captures the beauty of God's plan: Jesus becomes flesh and reveals God to us in a way we can understand.

Do you have a favorite Scripture verse? How did you come across it? Why is it your favorite?

Give the participants some time to share. Be sure to let them know this study is for folks who do not know much about the Bible just as much as it is for those who have been in study groups before. Remember we are all in this together.

4. John 1:14 helps us understand the emphasis of John's Gospel: Jesus reveals God to us because Jesus is, and always has been, God. That means He was God even before the beginning.

   God became flesh. As Catholics, we call that the Incarnation (God in the flesh). The Incarnation is unique to Christianity. No other religion makes the claim that God became flesh and dwelt among us. That is a bold Christian belief.

   The Gospel of John was originally written in Greek. When we look at "dwelt among us" in its original language, the phrase literally means God "pitched a tent among us," or "pitched His tabernacle among us." In Exodus 25:8–9, the tent or tabernacle represented God's presence among His people. God's glory resided in the tabernacle, much like He does today in our tabernacles for the Eucharist.

Do you believe Jesus truly is God in the flesh? How does belief in the Incarnation affect your life?

Encourage the participants to reflect for a moment on whether it really makes a difference for them that God became flesh when Jesus came. Christmas is the Feast of the Incarnation, when we celebrate that God became flesh. The Annunciation, which we celebrate on March 25, is when God announced His plan to Mary. You might share some of how it helps you to know that Jesus was completely human just like us. Therefore, He knows what our lives are like. And He can also show us the best way to live. He has been here.

If Jesus pitched His tent next door to your house or apartment, how would you react? What would you change about yourself, your life, or your residence?

You will probably want to go first in this sharing to set the stage for others to talk and feel comfortable.

5. The Prologue captures several big themes in the Gospel of John. Notice how John describes Jesus as light and truth. As you read John 1:1–18 in your Bible, underline "light" and "truth." These words will pop up more during your study.

6. John 1:12 reveals that Jesus is the link between heaven and earth. "But to all who received Him, who believed in His name, He gave power to become children of God . . ."

Jesus came to us, so we could come to Him.

Look later at John 1:51 and notice how Jesus is described very much the way Jacob's ladder is portrayed in Genesis 28:12, as connecting heaven and earth: "And he dreamed that there was a ladder set up on the earth, and the top of it reached to heaven; and behold, the angels of God were ascending and descending on it!"

What do you think about this image of Jesus? Can you envision Him connecting heaven and earth as the angels of God ascend and descend on Him?

This is a beautiful image, isn't it? Jesus links us to heaven. He is our gateway to God and to the eternal.

One saint who loved this idea of Jesus as linking heaven and earth was St. Catherine of Siena. She described Jesus as the Bridge in her famous writing *The Dialogue*. She shows how Jesus provides the bridge between death and life as He connects heaven and earth for us.

St. Catherine wrote of how the road to Heaven had been broken by the sin of Adam. To repair that, God made His Son a Bridge by which we humans could pass. I will share more about this Bridge in the DVD talk on this lesson.

Does it help you to see Jesus as the link between you and heaven? If yes, how so?

7. Look also at John 1:29 and 1:36. Circle the words "Lamb of God" in your Bible. Notice how John the Baptist describes Jesus as the "Lamb of God who takes away the sins of the world."

You probably recognize these words from the Mass. Why do you think we say these words right before we receive Communion?

When we celebrate the Eucharist, we receive the very Body and Blood of Jesus. His Blood takes away our sins in much the same way that the sacrificial lamb did for the Jews in the Old Testament. John the Baptist recognized that this was the role Jesus would play as the one who takes away our sins. The Book of Revelation teaches us all the saints in heaven sing to Jesus and call Him the "Lamb of God." Saying these words before receiving communion links us to Jesus in a fresh way each time we say them.

8. Read about the encounters Andrew and Philip had with Jesus in **John 1:40–42** and **John 1:45–46**.

   What do Andrew and Philip have in common?

   They both immediately told someone else about Jesus as soon as they encountered Him personally.

   How are they role models for us today? What do they teach us about being open to God and His plans?

   They immediately tell others about their encounter with Jesus and what they think it means. How do we share the faith with others?

If you have a few minutes remaining, you may want to ask the group about their own experiences when they completed Section IV: Personally Encountering Jesus. One or two participants might share how that exercise affected or helped them in seeking to meet Jesus in a new way. It might be especially meaningful for you to share some of your own experience here so that you model for the group what that encounter can look like.

If you do not have sufficient time, simply remind them that Section IV is designed to be very helpful in facilitating their own encounters with Jesus each week. "Be sure to take some time to complete that section. You'll be glad you did."

SESSION THREE

THE WEDDING PARTY ENCOUNTERS JESUS

KEY VERSE:

This, the first of His signs, Jesus did at Cana in Galilee, and manifested His glory; and His disciples believed in Him. (John 2:11)

II. This Week's Encounter—John 2:1–11

These verses share the story of Jesus' first miracle—turning water into wine at the wedding at Cana.

Answer the following questions to help you reflect on what you have read in John 2:1–11. **Tip: Circle the questions you find the most interesting or difficult and discuss them with your group at the next session.**

1. John doesn't provide any details about how the bride and groom reacted "when the wine failed . . ." (John 2:3). In fact, the Gospel doesn't specifically say that the bride and groom even knew about the situation. We do know that the wedding servers discovered that the wine was gone.

   Describe how the bride and groom might have felt "when the wine failed."

   This can be a fun conversation about possible feelings and reactions to what it was like to be in the Gospel story. Allow the group to imagine and have a creative conversation about this miracle at Cana.

   Have you ever been present for a wedding that had a huge embarrassing moment?

   How do you think the wedding servers felt?

2. When the wine runs short, Mary doesn't hesitate—she immediately turns to Jesus and says, "They have no wine." Notice that Mary's first instinct was to turn to Jesus when the wine ran out.

Even though we will discuss Mary in more detail later in the study, this may prompt helpful reflection in the group regarding Mary and her special place in Jesus' life and in our lives.

Jesus responds, "O woman, what have you to do with me? My hour has not yet come" (John 2:4). That almost sounds disrespectful, doesn't it? But that's not the case. During Jesus' time, the term "woman" was a common and polite way to address a woman. In fact, Jesus uses it again when He speaks to Mary from the cross in John 19:26.

Here, Jesus' response really means, "Why is this wine shortage any of *our* business?"

Why do you think Jesus responded like He did?

3. We will talk more about Mary, the Mother of God, later in this study. For now, consider whether you have had a time in your life when you asked Mary to help you. Perhaps it was a time you prayed a Hail Mary.

Is it helpful for you to think about her asking Jesus to help you just like she did for the bride and groom in this story? They had a shortage, and Mary intervened and asked Jesus to help.

Is there an area of your life right now where you'd like to experience an abundance rather than a shortage? How might Mary intercede with Jesus for you?

Again, we will discuss Mary in greater detail later. However, it is OK to spend a few minutes here reflecting on her role in helping us to meet Jesus personally.

4. This is our key verse for the session:

   This, the first of His signs, Jesus did at Cana in Galilee, and manifested His glory; and His disciples believed in Him. (John 2:11)

   Jesus performs seven signs in the first half of the Fourth Gospel. If time permits, quickly read each of the additional six "sign" stories. Make note of what kind of shortage Jesus addresses in these six additional signs. Focus on how He turns shortages into abundance.

   - John 4:46-54—Healing the official's son
   - John 5:1-15—Healing the lame man by the pool of Bethsaida
   - John 6:1-14—Feeding of five thousand people
   - John 6: 16-20—Walking on water
   - John 9:1-41—Healing the man born blind
   - John 11:34-44—Raising Lazarus from the dead

5. God's Glory

   John 2:11 says the signs reveal Jesus' glory.

   Remember from last week's session: "And the Word became flesh and dwelt among us, full of grace and truth; we have beheld His glory," (John 1:14). This means that we see the glory of God in Jesus. Jesus is God's presence among us.

When you think of God's glory, what comes to mind? How would you describe God's glory in your own words?

Reassure the group that none of us can fully explain or understand the glory of God. His glory is His supreme splendor and magnificence. In paragraph 300 of the Catechism, the Church teaches:

> God is infinitely greater than all his works: "You have set your glory above the heavens." Indeed, God's "greatness is unsearchable" . . . In the words of St. Augustine, God is "higher than my highest and more inward than my innermost self."

At the same time, it is important to consider the majesty and glory of God who is divine and eternal. He is preparing us to be in that glorious presence someday.

When you receive the Eucharist, do you ever pause and reflect that the glory of God is entering you through the Body and Blood of Jesus, the Word made flesh?

Does that make you feel differently about the sacrament of the Eucharist?

Encourage the group to pause and reflect for a moment on just how special this makes the Eucharist. What a gift God has given us! A powerful way to experience this is to stop and gaze at the crucifix when you receive communion. Ponder God's immense glory for just a moment as you receive His body and blood.

6. After this first sign, "His disciples believed in Him" (John 2:11).

Do you think it would be easier to believe in Jesus if you witnessed one or more of His signs, or miracles?

Read John 6:30; 7:31; and 12:37. Why do you think so many people struggled to believe in Jesus, even after they had seen Him?

We like to think that it would be so easy if we could have just seen Jesus along with the disciples. But, clearly, it was not that easy then either. The disciples struggled to believe two thousand years ago just as we still struggle at times today.

Do you remember the story of Thomas, often called Doubting Thomas? (If not, feel free to read John 20:24–29.) Thomas refused to believe that Jesus had been raised from the dead until he saw the risen Jesus for himself. Like many people, Thomas thought that seeing is believing. Can you identify with Thomas?

Why do you personally believe in Jesus?

This question may be a little intimidating for some participants, especially for those who are new to the faith or are sharing in a group for the first time. As the leader, you might help make this discussion most useful by going first and briefly sharing why you believe. You might also know one person in the group who will answer this question well and call on them. This question will prompt everyone to take a moment to reflect on what and why they believe, and that is the goal of the study: to discover Jesus and grow in our faith in Him.

Do you ever struggle with your faith in Jesus?

Reassure the group that our conversations are private and that no one will share outside the group. We are here for each other. We all have struggles, and we are all praying for each other during the week. This is the perfect time to examine our struggles and try to grow past them.

In what area of your life do you struggle most with putting your faith in Jesus?

How can the story of the wedding servers and the bride and groom help you to deepen your faith?

Notes

SESSION FOUR:

NICODEMUS ENCOUNTERS JESUS

KEY VERSE:

This man came to Jesus by night and said to Him,
"Rabbi, we know that you are a teacher come from God;
for no one can do these signs that you do,
unless God is with him."
(John 3:2)

II. This Week's Encounter—John 3:1–21

These verses reveal Nicodemus' encounter with Jesus.

Answer the following questions to help you reflect on what you read in John 3:1–21. **Tip: Circle the questions you find the most interesting or difficult and discuss them with your group at the next session.**

1. In John 3:2, Nicodemus "came to Jesus by night." What are some reasons Nicodemus may have visited Jesus when it was dark?

   Here are two possibilities to consider: Perhaps Nicodemus was scared of being seen by the opponents of Jesus. Perhaps he was embarrassed that, as a religious leader, he did not understand who Jesus was and needed to ask more questions.

2. Throughout his Gospel, John uses day/night and light/dark imagery. Take a look at these verses from John and make a brief note on what John is saying in each.

   - John 1:5
   - John 3:2
   - John 3:19–21
   - John 8:12
   - John 11:10
   - John 12:36
   - John 12:46
   - John 13:30
   - John 19:39

3. Nicodemus wants to know more about Jesus. He has seen some of the signs and is trying to figure out the truth about who Jesus is. Jesus responds to Nicodemus in John 3:3 with the words, "Unless one is born anew, he cannot see the kingdom of God."

   The Greek word for *anew* or *again* can also be translated *above*. Since in John 3:31, Jesus is clearly speaking about coming from above, verse 3 is often translated "born from above."

   What do you think Jesus means by the statement "Unless one is born anew, he cannot see the kingdom of God"?

   We require God's help in order to become the people He desires us to be. We certainly cooperate with God to become the-best-versions-of-ourselves. However, it is God who supplies the power. It is His grace that allows us to see Him and to see our lives differently.

   TIP: Look at John 1:12–13 and John 8:23 for additional thoughts on this idea.

4. In John 3:5–8, Jesus expands on the idea of "being born anew." He contrasts being "born of flesh" with "being born of water and Spirit."

   Take a quick look at these verses found later in the New Testament

   - Romans 6:4
   - 1 Corinthians 6:11
   - 1 Corinthians 12:13
   - Titus 3:5–6

What do you think it means to be "born of water and Spirit"?

Here Jesus contrasts "born of the Spirit" with "born of the flesh." The world sees things only through the flesh. But with God's help, believers see things spiritually, through the eyes of God. When He says "born of water," Jesus probably is referring to baptism as a defining time in our lives. Baptism is the gateway to a spiritual life. It is then that we are given the Spirit of God. Paragraphs 1213 and 1215 of the Catechism provide more of the Church's teaching on this.

5. You are probably familiar with the famous words of John 3:16. "For God so loved *the world* that He gave His only Son, that *whoever* believes in Him should not perish but have eternal life."

These words reinforce what we learned about the theme of the Gospel found in John 20:31. Jesus came to give us life.

Do this exercise as a group.

Take a moment and substitute your name in place of "the world" in the words of this famous verse.

"For God so loved **[YOUR NAME]** that He gave His only Son, that **[YOUR NAME]** who believes in Him should not perish but have eternal life."

How does it make you feel to say these words aloud?

Does it help you experience the love God has for you? How so?

If possible, have each person say this aloud one at a time, using his or her own name. Doing this will help the participants experience the love of God individually in their own lives.

6. Read John 3:17. Coming after John 3:16, this verse is often forgotten. Underline John 3:17 in your Bible. Circle the words "not" and "condemn." Let this remind you of God's love. He doesn't want to condemn you (or anyone in the world)—He wants to love and save all people.

   How does John 3:17 affect your understanding of John 3:16?

7. Nicodemus shows up two more times later in the Gospel of John.

   Read John 7:45–52. What does this passage say about Nicodemus?

   Read John 19:38–42. What does this passage say about Nicodemus?

   How do you see Nicodemus growing and changing as the Gospel story unfolds?

The exercise in Section IV on Personal Encounter points out that Nicodemus seems to be moving closer and closer to Jesus. In each of the three times he appears in the Gospel of John, Nicodemus is a bit more bold about who Jesus is.

Notes

SESSION FIVE:

TWO WAYWARD WOMEN ENCOUNTER JESUS

KEY VERSE:

And Jesus said, "Neither do I condemn you; go, and do not sin again." (John 8:11)

II. This Week's Encounters—John 4:4–42 and 8:1–11

These passages share the stories of two wayward yet remarkable women who encounter Jesus and experience His mercy and forgiveness.

Answer the following questions to help you reflect on what you read in John 4:4–42 and John 8:1–11. **Tip: Circle the questions you find most interesting or difficult and discuss them with your group at the next session.**

1. In John 4:4–42, Jesus talks to an unnamed Samaritan woman at a well in Sychar, a town in Samaria. This conversation is very unexpected for several reasons.

    - **She is a woman.** During Jesus' time, Jewish teachers weren't supposed to speak with women in public. But Jesus meets her in a public place in broad daylight at noon.

    - **She is a Samaritan.** Jews and Samaritans had long-standing hostility for one another. A Jewish teacher would have refused to drink from a vessel used by a Samaritan, yet Jesus treats this woman with dignity.

    - **She has a well-known, tainted past.** She was married far more than three times, which was the absolute legal limit for Jewish marriages at the time. That is probably why she was fetching water in the middle of the day when most people would have been doing other things.

    In other words, the Samaritan woman at the well is the wrong gender, wrong race, wrong religion, and in the wrong moral standing. Nevertheless, Jesus has a public conversation with her.

Describe a person today who would be equivalent in our culture's eyes to this woman. Can you envision Jesus speaking with him or her?

Good examples of this might be a prostitute or an exotic dancer whom everyone considers to be of little value,

or a beggar on the street whom everyone else avoids,

or a Muslim person whom many people would prefer to ignore,

or a relative who has hurt the family,

or perhaps a child with Down Syndrome, in a culture that aborts 90 percent of children who have been diagnosed with that condition.

2. In John 4:10, Jesus makes it clear that He wants to give the Samaritan woman a gift.

   Take a look later in the New Testament at these verses in the short letters of John which may have also been written by the same John who wrote the Fourth Gospel.

   - 1 John 4:9–10
   - 1 John 4:19

   What kind of gift do you think Jesus has in mind? What is motivating Jesus?

3. In John 4:24-26, Jesus teaches the Samaritan woman that those who worship Him "must worship in Spirit and truth." What do you think He means?

   Tip: The following verses might also help you interpret Jesus' words to the woman:

   - John 1:14, 17, 33
   - John 3:5-8
   - John 8:31-32
   - John 17:17-19
   - John 18:37
   - John 20:22

   The Spirit is the spirit given by God. That Spirit reveals the Truth to us and allows us to worship God in the right fashion. He is the source of our spiritual lives and He gives us the Truth.

4. In John 4:28-30, the woman leaves her water jar and runs to tell crowds of other people what she has just encountered with Jesus.

   Has a highly unlikely person ever taught you about Jesus, God, or faith? Did you give attention to his or her words? Why or why not?

   The woman runs and tells other people what has happened to her. It seems likely that a lot of people would not be willing to listen to her because they had already given up on her. But she now has a lot to say, given that she has encountered Jesus and had such a lengthy conversation with Him. Are you open to listening to other people, who may be very different from you, when they may have something to say about Jesus and the faith?

5. In John 8:1-11, Jesus meets another woman with a questionable reputation. She has been caught in adultery. What are the differences between this story and the story in John 4:4-42 about the woman at the well?

There are many possible answers. Some might include:
The people are ready to stone the adulteress to death. Jesus confronts the crowd rather than just having an individual conversation. Jesus is very specific in his instructions to the adulterous woman.

6. Read the following Old Testament verses. What is the law concerning adultery?

   - Leviticus 20:10
   - Deuteronomy 17:6-7
   - Deuteronomy 22:22

7. This is our key verse for the lesson:

   And Jesus said, "Neither do I condemn you; go, and do not sin again." (John 8:11)

   These are life-giving, life-changing words. Jesus forgives her and offers her a future. This is what redemption looks like.

   Compare this story to what St. Paul writes in 1 Thessalonians 5:23-24. How does this passage give deeper meaning to the story of the adulterous woman? What is Jesus doing?

God has big plans for each of us. He calls us to holiness. He promises to help us achieve that. God's power can transform any of us into the-best-version-of-ourselves.

In the same way, what do you believe God hopes and plans to do in your own life?

This is an important question to ask yourself. What does God want in my life? Where am I headed?

8. What do the powerful stories about the Samaritan woman and the adulterous woman teach us about Jesus?

There are many great answers for this. Some would include the following:

- *There is no one outside the reach or love of Jesus.*
- *Jesus has big things in mind for every life because each of us is made in His image.*
- *Jesus cares more about your future than He does about your past.*
- *Jesus changes us. He desires to make you a-better-version-of-yourself. He doesn't leave us in our sin but takes us to a place of greater holiness.*

SESSION SIX:

HUNGRY CROWDS ENCOUNTER JESUS

KEY VERSE:

He who eats my flesh and drinks my blood abides in me, and I in him. (John 6:56)

II. This Week's Encounter···John 6:22–69

This passage, found after Jesus miraculously feeds five thousand people with five loaves and two fish and walks on the water, contains some of the most powerful and significant words of the Gospel and the Catholic faith.

Answer the following questions to help you reflect on what you read in John 6:22–69. **Tip: Circle the questions you find most interesting or difficult and discuss them with your group at the next session.**

1. John 6:22–69 is a long passage. What three things most fascinate you or most capture your attention?

2. This passage is loaded with references to the Old Testament. Compare the following Old Testament passages with the teachings in John chapter six. What do you notice?

   - Exodus 16:2–4 *The Israelites question God's capacity to feed them.*
   - Psalms 78:23–25 *The psalms praise God for His abundant provision.*
   - Numbers 11:11–13 *Moses wonders how he can provide food for the people.*
   - 2 Kings 4:42–44 *Elisha the prophet performs a miraculous feeding with God's help.*

3. Jesus often appears to repeat Himself in John 6:22-69. Note briefly what He says in each of the following verses:

    - John 6:35
    - John 6:48
    - John 6:51
    - John 6:53
    - John 6:54
    - John 6:55
    - John 6:56 (our key verse this week)
    - John 6:57
    - John 6:58

    Why do you think Jesus emphasizes these points so much?

    This must be a really important teaching. Jesus repeatedly emphasizes the importance and significance of the Eucharist. His presence is real.

    Do you see a relationship between the above verses and John 1:14?

    Jesus became flesh. Now He gives us His flesh that we might encounter Him and be nourished by Him always.

4. In John 6:11, Jesus gave thanks. In Greek, the word for "thanksgiving" is *eucharisto*, which is where we get the English word "Eucharist." When we celebrate the Eucharist, we give thanks to God.

Compare Jesus' actions in John 6:11 to His words at the Last Supper in Luke 22:19. What do you notice?

Notice the remarkable similarities between how Jesus treats the bread in feeding the crowd in John and in feeding the disciples at the Last Supper in Luke. He takes the bread, gives thanks, breaks it, and gives it to the people.

5. In John 6:56, Jesus makes a bold promise.

    Read John 15:4-7 for an expansion of Jesus' promise. In your own words, describe the promise.

    Take a look at John 14:23 and John 17:21-23. How do they further expand Jesus' promise?

    Jesus is inviting us into the most intimate, connected relationship with Him imaginable. He is inviting us into a loving union with God in the Trinity. That union is eternal. This is a really bold promise!

6. Read John 6:60-66 again. Why do you think so many disciples turn away and leave Jesus at this point?

    Many people today are confused by what the Church teaches about the Eucharist. It only makes sense that many would have been confused then when Jesus first described eating His flesh and drinking His blood. Some found it so difficult to comprehend that they abandoned Jesus altogether.

Are there parts of Jesus' life and teachings that you find difficult to understand or obey?

For you, what is the hardest part of being a follower of Jesus?

Again, this type of question may be a little intimidating for some participants, especially for those who are new to the faith or are sharing in a group for the first time. As the leader, like before, you might help make this discussion most useful by going first and briefly sharing what is hard for you. Perhaps you have friends who avoid you because of your faith, or perhaps being a Christian makes you uncomfortable at work. Maybe giving money is difficult for you or making time to serve the poor. You might also know one person in the group who will answer this question well and call on them. This question will prompt everyone to take a moment to reflect on what and why they believe, and that is the goal of the study: to discover Jesus and grow in our faith in Him.

7. In John 6:67, Jesus asks the Twelve, "Do you also wish to go away?" What does Peter's response mean to you?

   Have you ever felt the way Peter did, as though you had no one else to go to except Jesus? If so, describe that time in your life.

This is a good time to remind the group of the power of Section III in each lesson—Just for You: Experiencing Jesus.

Encourage them to live out the lessons each week by utilizing that section. Coupled with the group sessions, this personalized section is where a deep, true encounter with Christ can emerge.

Notes

SESSION SEVEN:

LAZARUS, MARTHA, AND MARY ENCOUNTER JESUS

KEY VERSE:

When He had said this, He cried in a loud voice, "Lazarus, come out!" (John 11:43)

II. This Week's Encounter—John 11:1–12:11

This long passage shares Martha, Mary, and Lazarus' encounter with Jesus. It is the last of Jesus' seven signs and sets the stage for the Passion narrative.

Answer the following questions to help you digest what you read in John 11:1—12:11. **Tip: Circle the questions you find most interesting or difficult and discuss them with your group at the next session.**

1. St. Ignatius of Loyola liked to read Scripture and meditate on it by imagining himself present in the story. Place yourself in this story, either as one of the characters or as a spectator watching the events unfold. Jesus arrives when Lazarus has already been in the tomb for four days. Describe the scene, the smells and the sounds of the village, the mourners, the cemetery, Jesus' disciples, and Mary and Martha. What are some of the emotions and feelings that those at the scene are experiencing?

   This method of imaginatively placing yourself in the Biblical story produced great fruit in the life of St. Ignatius. Provide the group some time to really allow their creativity to flow in thinking about this story using this technique. They probably will find this experience very helpful not only in this discussion but in their future reading of Scripture.

2. In this story, we encounter a Jesus who fully experiences human emotions and reactions. Read the following verses.

   - John 11:33
   - John 11:35
   - John 11:38

What do these verses tell us about Jesus?

There may be many good answers to this question, but it is clear that Jesus operates with a full range of human emotions. Few of us really ever consider that fact.

3. When Martha and Mary send word to Jesus about their ill brother, Lazarus, Jesus takes His time traveling to Bethany to see his sick friend. Jesus clearly acts on His own time.

   Have you ever waited on Jesus to answer a prayer?

   If so, what was that experience of waiting on Jesus like? Did it make you trust Him more or less?

   Again, this personal question will probably best be discussed if you as the leader first share something from your own experience. Most people have experienced this waiting on an answer to prayer, but it is often not discussed. This discussion will likely bear fruit in most of the participants' spiritual lives, even those who remain silent during the group session.

   For example, you might have experienced something like this:

   My friend Tina prayed for her stepfather for thirty years before he ever expressed an interest in the faith and the Church. Those thirty years were hard, but something happened when he came to attend a family member's baptism, and that sparked him to rediscover his faith.

4. Martha boldly responds to Jesus after He asks her, "Whoever lives and believes in me shall never die. Do you believe this?" (John 11:26).

   What do you think about Martha's response to Jesus in John 11:27?

   Compare her response to that of Peter in John 6:67–69.

   How do you think you would have responded to Jesus' question in John 11:26? "Whoever lives and believes in me shall never die. Do you believe this?"

5. Jesus risks His own life to give life to Lazarus. Read John 3:16–17 and John 10:14–18 again. How do you see all these passages fitting together?

   There will be a lot of good answers to this question. One good observation would be that Jesus gives life—from the very beginning at Creation, through giving life to Lazarus from the dead, and even giving His own life from beginning to end on behalf of the world.

6. In the Nicene Creed, we say we "believe in the Holy Spirit, the Lord, **the Giver of Life**."

   Here, in chapter eleven, **Jesus gives life** to Lazarus in our key verse:

   When He had said this, He cried in a loud voice,
   "Lazarus, come out!"
   (John 11:43)

In John 1:2–4, all things came to be through the Word and what came to be through Him was life.

In Genesis chapters one and two (look at Genesis 1:24 and 2:7), **God the Father creates life**.

Notice how all three persons of the Trinity are involved in giving life. Father. Son. Holy Spirit. Our God is a life-giver.

What does the phrase "Giver of Life" mean to you?

List some specific ways you have experienced, are experiencing, or hope to experience God's giving life to you.

7. In many ways, the resurrection stories of Lazarus and Jesus define the Christian faith. Someone once said, "If you don't believe in the resurrection, then you're not a believer." What do you think that statement means?

In the New Testament, we discover that Jesus appeared in His post-resurrection form twelve times in the six weeks after Easter. He appeared to the apostles several times, He also appeared to two disciples walking on the road to Emmaus. He even appeared to five hundred people at one time (see 1 Corinthians 15:6).

Do you struggle, or is it easy for you to believe in the resurrection of Jesus?

The Church teaches that we will all be raised from the dead at the end of time. Paragraph 1017 of the *Catechism of the Catholic Church* reminds us: "We believe in the true resurrection of this flesh that we now possess . . . We sow a corruptible body in the tomb, but he raises up an incorruptible body, a 'spiritual body' . . ."

How does the story of Lazarus help you?

Pope Francis said in a general audience address in April 2013, "It is precisely the Resurrection that offers us the greatest hope because it opens our lives and the life of the world to God's eternal future, to complete happiness, to the certainty that evil, sin, and death can be conquered. This leads us to living our everyday lives more confidently, to facing each day courageously and with commitment. Christ's Resurrection shines new light on our everyday realities. Christ's Resurrection is our strength!"

In other words, we are Easter people.

Do your beliefs in the resurrection affect the way you live your life? How so?

Encourage the participants to reflect for a moment on whether it really makes a difference for them that Jesus was raised from the dead. You might share some of how it helps you to know that Jesus conquered death and still lives today at the right hand of God the Father. Therefore, He is active in heaven, and on earth in our lives. There is real power in knowing and embracing that. Again, it may be helpful to point the group to Section IV which is designed this week to help them personally experience that power.

SESSION EIGHT:

PETER ENCOUNTERS JESUS

KEY VERSE:

He came to Simon Peter; and Peter said to Him, "Lord, do you wash my feet?" (John 13:6)

II. This week's Encounter—John 13:1-38

This passage shares Peter's encounter with Jesus and is full of failure, disappointment, redemption, and leadership.

Answer the following questions to help you digest what you read in John 13:1-38. **Tip: Circle the questions you find most interesting or difficult and discuss them with your group at the next session.**

1. Chapter thirteen begins the Book of Glory, the second half of John which describes Jesus' farewell teachings to the disciples and the story of His Passion, death and resurrection. Read the following verses. Write down what you see as the key theme and purpose for each farewell teaching.

    - John 13:1, 34; 15:12-13

      Jesus' famous commandment to love one another

    - John 14:1-6

      Jesus promises a future and a home in heaven

    - John 14:15-17

      Jesus assures them of the continuing presence of God in the Holy Spirit

    - John 17:20-24

      Jesus prays for unity in His followers and disciples. That unity is based on the unity of the three persons in the Trinity

2. John 13:1–20 is John's description of the Last Supper. How is this version different from the Last Supper story in the other Gospels? It may be helpful to read Matthew 26:17–24 or Luke 22:7–23 for a comparison.

Notice how the Gospel of John focuses primarily on Jesus' washing of His disciples' feet while the other Gospels have the more familiar emphasis on the bread and wine being offered as the body of Christ. Remember how John emphasized the Eucharist in John chapter six.

3. Unlike Matthew's, Mark's, and Luke's accounts, John's Last Supper story emphasizes how Jesus washes His disciples' feet.

   Considering how unusual and shocking this would have been during Jesus' time, why do you think Jesus chose to do that humiliating act?

   There are many helpful ways to understand this. One would be that Jesus is showing them the same love He has commanded them to have in loving one another. A second way would be to see His providing a model of what it means to be a true servant leader.

   Can you think of any examples of modern leaders performing a comparable act or leading with a "servant" attitude?

   E.g., Pope Francis offers many examples in his own leadership: from choosing not to live in the papal apartments, to traveling in simple cars, to spending large amounts of time with people in great need.

Describe the best example of servant leadership you have personally witnessed in the past week.

Perhaps you work for a boss who closed the office for a day so the whole team could serve the poor or attend a funeral of a colleague. Or perhaps you have a mother who is especially selfless.

4. This is our key verse for the week:

   He came to Simon Peter; and Peter said to Him,
   "Lord, do you wash my feet?"
   (John 13:6)

   Why do you think Peter resists and feels uncomfortable with Jesus washing His disciples' feet (**John 13:6–10**)?

   For many people, being served feels uncomfortable. For Peter, how much more so must it have felt to be served like that by Jesus, the Son of God?

   Have you ever been served by someone and felt humbled by it? If so, how did you respond?

5. Not long after the Last Supper and foot-washing, Peter denies Jesus three times.

   Read **John 13:36–38**; **John 18:15–18**; and **John 18:25–27**.

   Have you ever had an embarrassing failure? Did other people know about it? Describe what that felt like. How did you try to overcome that failure and move forward?

6. Now read John 20:1-10. What do you notice about Peter as he goes to the empty tomb?

Even though Peter has denied Jesus and failed, he is eager to discover what has happened at the tomb. He is still clinging to Jesus in spite of his three denials of Him.

7. After Peter goes to the empty tomb, he only appears one more time in John's Gospel. Read John 21:1-19 and describe Peter's role in Jesus' resurrection appearance to His disciples.

What does Jesus say to Peter? Why do you think Jesus says these things to Peter?

In many ways, Jesus is restoring Peter. After all, Peter denied Jesus three times. Here, Jesus pronounces His blessing on Peter three times and charges Peter with a new mission three times (Feed my lambs, Tend my sheep, Feed my sheep). Jesus is rehabilitating Peter and sending him forward to lead the Church.

How do you think Peter feels as Jesus speaks to him?

Notes

SESSION NINE:

MARY ENCOUNTERS JESUS

KEY VERSE:

Then He said to the disciple, "Behold, your mother!" And from that hour the disciple took her to his own home. (John 19:27)

II. This Week's Encounter—John 19:25-30

These verses record Jesus' last words to His mother, His last breath, and His death on the cross.

Answer the following questions to help you digest what you read in John 19:25-30. **Tip: Circle the questions that are most interesting or difficult for you so that you can explore these more when your group discussion occurs at the next session.**

1. All of chapter nineteen focuses on the crucifixion of Jesus. It will be helpful to read the whole chapter and notice the details John provides as he shares this painful story.

   John 19:17—Jesus carries the cross Himself. He is alone.

   John 19:19-20—Pilate places an inscription on the cross, written in three languages: Greek (the dominant language of the day, particularly used in commerce), Hebrew (the language of the Jews, particularly used in religious matters), and Latin (the language of the Roman Empire and the language of legal affairs). It is from this inscription that we get "INRI," usually inscribed on crucifixes in Catholic parishes. These four letters represent the first letter of each Latin word in "Jesus of Nazareth, the King of the Jews."

   John 19:24—John's Gospel refers to Psalms 22:19 to explain why the soldiers cast lots for Jesus' seamless tunic.

   John 19:30—Jesus bows His head and "gave up His spirit." This can be understood in two ways. First, Jesus gives up the spirit of His earthly existence. In other words, He dies with that last breath. Second, Jesus hands over the Holy Spirit to His believers. Take a look at John 7:39; 14:15-20; 14:25-29; and 20:21-23.

John 19:30—In Greek, Jesus' last word is tetelestai, which is translated, "It is finished." This single Greek word can also be translated, "It is complete," or, "It is perfected." For more depth, look at the use of the same word in John 4:34; 5:36; and 17:4.

Now that you have read the entire Gospel of John, what do you think Jesus means by this final word?

Again, there are many ways to understand this statement. But it seems likely that Jesus views His mission here on earth to now be complete. He may also be saying that His act of saving us and leading us to God has now been perfected, or perfectly accomplished.

2. Imagine you are Mary, the Mother of Jesus. Place yourself in this story—you are standing at the foot of the cross and witnessing the death of your only son. You are faithful all the way to the end. Describe the scene Mary witnesses. Try to imagine the memories she is recalling. Consider how Mary feels and the emotions that come to the surface.

3. This is our key verse for the week:

Then He said to the disciple, 'Behold, your mother!'
And from that hour the disciple took her to his own home.
(John 19:27)

In John 19:25-27, in His last moments, Jesus entrusts Mary, His mother, to His beloved disciple. Although John's Gospel never explicitly names the beloved disciple, it is believed that he is likely John the Apostle, the author of the Fourth Gospel. But his identity is not as important as the act itself.

Jesus hands His own mother, Mary, over to the disciple and to the Church. Tradition says that Mary went to live with John, and stayed with him during the time he oversaw the churches in Asia from his home near Ephesus. Pilgrims still visit that home site each year, especially since Mary may have spent her final days on earth there.

What does this action of Jesus mean to you?

Do you consider Mary to be your Mother as a believer?

4. Mary is the mother of the Church and the mother of us all.

Return now to the first time we meet Mary in the Fourth Gospel. Review the story of the wedding in Cana of Galilee (John 2:1-11). Notice how Jesus addresses Mary in the same way (as "woman") in both stories (see John 2:4 and 19:26). This term is a normal, respectful way of addressing a woman at that time.

Notice also that at Cana (John 2:4) Jesus says His hour has not yet come. In John chapter nineteen, His hour has clearly arrived. In fact, it began in John 13:1. The hour of Jesus' glorification has arrived. That's because it is in the cross, not in any sign or miracle, that we encounter Jesus most deeply. At the cross, His sacrifice is made complete.

As you read John chapter two again, notice how Mary intercedes when the wedding party runs out of wine. She knows that Jesus can do something about that shortage. Jesus' mother knows what Jesus can do, and she can encourage Him to do that. She is the Mother of God.

Do you see Mary as your intercessor? As your advocate? As someone who will encourage Jesus to help you and love you? Why or why not?

Remember that for some people this relationship with Mary will be more foreign than for others. For those who grew up in homes with a deep devotion to Mary, she has been at the center of their lives for many years. For others, who may have grown up in non-active families or in Protestant settings, discussing Mary will be a newer experience. This will be a time of discovery and possibly even question-asking. Encourage that exploration in your discussion.

Have there been moments in your life when you have felt or seen Mary's presence or help? If so, describe one of those moments.

5. Mary has many names and titles. Here are just a few of the ways we address her.

    - Mother of Christ
    - Mother of divine grace
    - Mother most pure
    - Mother undefiled
    - Mother most amiable
    - Mother most admirable
    - Mother of good counsel
    - Mother of our Creator
    - Mother of our Savior
    - Ark of the covenant
    - Gate of heaven

Do you have a name or title for Mary that is especially meaningful to you? If so, why is that name special?

Invite the participants to be open and real as they discuss Mary. Be sure to allow time for anyone who wishes to speak to do so, rather than letting one or two participants who may have a particularly strong interest in Mary dominate.

6. Often, our relationships with our own family, particularly with our mother and father, shape our relationship with God. Reflect on how this may or may not be true in your own relationships with your parents and with God. Do you see any connections between how you related to your mother or father with how you relate to God or to Mary?

7. In this story, we also encounter "the other disciple," or the "beloved disciple." It seems most likely that he is the apostle John, the author of this Fourth Gospel. Take a look at the passages listed below and think about this fascinating character in the Gospel. He had his own very powerful experiences with Jesus, and those experiences form the foundation of his writing.

   - John 13:23–25
   - John 18:15–16
   - John 19:26–27
   - John 20:1–10
   - John 21:7, 20–24

NOTE: If you would like to explore further the Gospel of John and its history—author, setting, dates, and other details—please visit **dynamiccatholic.com/exploreJohn** to receive a short list of helpful scholarly resources.

V. Moving Forward

Congratulations! You've read the entire Gospel of John, studied it, and discovered a wide variety of people who met Jesus.

Try to save some time for these closing questions. They will be very helpful in summarizing this experience and exploring what a good next step for each person will be. As you close this session, be sure to encourage the participants to complete this section if they have not already done so. Let them know that you want to be sure their journey with Christ continues to advance and grow.

1. How has this experience shaped your own journey and experience of Jesus?

2. What is one excellent next step you can take to deepen your faith and love for Jesus? What's the next right thing to do? How can you make this next step a reality?

3. This nine-week journey has helped you experience Jesus. Early in our study, we discovered how Philip and Andrew helped lead other people to Jesus (John 1:40-46). What is one thing you can do to help another person encounter Jesus?

Here are some ideas to get you started:

- Pray specifically each day for one person you know who would benefit from an encounter with Jesus.

- Share a copy of your favorite faith-centered book with another person. Free and low-cost resources for this can be found at **dynamiccatholic.com/MyTurningPoint**.

- Form a new small group and lead the participants through this Gospel of John study, *The Turning Point*.

ADDITIONAL RESOURCES

for your PRAYER LIFE as you JOURNEY through the GOSPEL of JOHN

The Dynamic Catholic Prayer Process

Here is the basic Prayer Process that our team at Dynamic Catholic uses and suggests as a starting point for building your own prayer relationship with God. Matthew Kelly developed this simple process after studying hundreds of prayer styles and disciplines from many Catholic spiritualities. Again, the point is forming a simple, regular habit, five to ten minutes a day. Daily prayer IS your relationship with God.

1. Gratitude - Begin by thanking God in a personal dialogue for whatever you are most grateful for today.

2. Awareness - Revisit the times in the past twenty-four hours when you were and were not the-best-version-of-yourself. Talk to God about these situations and ask Him to give you the gift of greater awareness when similar situations arise in the future.

3. Significant Moments - Identify something you experienced today and explore what God might be trying to say to you through that event.

4. Peace - Ask God to forgive you for any wrong you have committed (against yourself, another person, or Him) and fill you with a deep and abiding peace.

5. Freedom - Talk to God about how He is inviting you to change your life so you can experience the freedom that comes from knowing that who you are, where you are, and what you are doing makes sense. Is He inviting you to rethink the way you do things? Is God asking you to let go of something or someone? Is He asking you to hold on to something or someone?

6. Pray for Others - Pray for those you feel called to pray for today, and those who have asked you to pray for them recently. Take a moment and pray for these people by name, asking God to bless and guide them.

Finish by praying the Our Father.

Mary

I have always imagined you to be young
With serene beauty
Sun-kissed face that searched the heavens
With questions only deep
Within your heart
With great love you carried your child
Watching Him grow beneath the
moon of Israel
And under Egypt's stars

You took the splinters from His
dusty hands
Turning wood on Joseph's bench
And held Him close when he spoke
of things
You could only carry in your heart

Did you know what lay ahead?
How He would heal the sick
Raise the dead
Find the lost and
See the hungry fed?
Little children would be well again
The blind would see
Lazarus would rise
And the lame run free

Did you know that your heart
would break?
When He was bound and beaten
Hung upon a tree
For all the world to see
The sin of humanity
Did your heart almost burst
When you heard the tomb was empty?
Did you run to see
And cry again so many tears of joy?

In Heaven you do not age
And you are forever young
You are beautiful
Because you love
May we know that love
In protection
In affection
In direction
Just as you watched over your own Son
Watch over us

Help us to find
That pure place in our heart
Beyond cynicism
Beyond hate
Beyond fear

Turn your gentle face towards us
That we might listen to your
Cana words
'Do as He tells you'

May we walk one day
When life is done
Through the fields of paradise
Forever young
Enfolded in your mystery
O woman clothed in the sun.

(Fr. Liam Lawton, *The Hope Prayer*)

Fr. Liam Lawton, *The Hope Prayer* (Chicago, IL: GIA Publications, 2010)

Jesus

I come before you
In these sacred moments
Opening the shutters of my heart
That You would call the light into the dark
The secret cavern of my soul

If I tell You who I am
Will you shelter me
Beneath the firm arms of your compassion
And gaze tenderly
Beyond the limits of my silence?

Who am I?

I am the son, the prodigal one
Returning from my journey
Of untold wrong
Where love was scarce
And temptation strong
Can You embrace me yet again?
I am the woman at the well
Tired and weary
Longing to quench my thirst
Drawing deep to find
Your truth as well

I am the blind one
By the pool of Siloam
Can You stir the waters so I will see
Your gentle eyes
That find the light in me?

I am the weak one
Waiting for years
But I knew You would come
So I might touch the hem of Your garment
And live again

I am the curious one
Gathering to listen with the crowd
Bringing bread and fish
That You break and bless
And all become Your guests

I am the sinner
They all know my sins
I see the stones
My accusers bring
What words You write in sand
One by one I see them stand
And walk away
From what is written on each heart

I am Lazarus, friend
Wrapped in the cloths of death
When You saw me
You wept
You have called me from my tomb
And I will live again

I am Nicodemus of the night
Preferring dark to light
You have sought me out
I long for life

I am the little child
Who lies in fever's sleep
I hear You call beyond death's reach
'Talitha Koum'
Little one – come forth

Your voice is more beautiful than the
Sweetest music
It resonates forever in my heart
I am all and I am more
I hear You knocking
On my door
Your lantern burning bright
Casting shadows where my life
Still seeks Your healing touch

Jesus
The beginning and the end
Jesus
I long to call you friend

(Fr. Liam Lawton, *The Hope Prayer*)[1]

1 Fr. Liam Lawton, *The Hope Prayer* (Chicago, IL: GIA Publications, 2010)

Notes

Notes